SURVIVE And THRIVE In The Coming Pension Fund Apocalypse

ISBN # 978-0-578-32279-7

Lee Rendel

TABLE OF CONTENTS

CHAPTER 1

QUICK OVERVIEW OF ECONOMICS

This book was intended to be a quick read and not a deep dive into macroeconomics, if your only interest is to know how to protect yourself and your family go directly to chapter 6 but if instead, you are interested in basic economics and how the U.S. got into this situation you can start here.

The Economy

An Economy is based on Goods and Services the more goods and services an economy has in relation to its debt, the stronger the economy.

When the debt to GDP (Gross Domestic Product) of a nation goes over 90%, it's nearly impossible to pay back the debt because you only have 10% of growth to pay back the 90% of the debt. At the end of the first quarter of 2021, the debt-to-GDP ratio of the U.S. stood at 127%.

After World War 2, and into the 1950's and 60's, the U.S. had one of the strongest economies ever in the history of the world. With a massive manufacturing base, with names such as General Motors, Ford, Chrysler, and Boeing, just to name a few.

These manufacturers had engineers and machinists that were tested during the war to go from manufacturing cars to manufacturing tanks, and sometimes airplanes in the course of a little over a year.

After the war, we had massive manufacturing capacity. Countries in Europe and elsewhere, who had lost their manufacturing plants during the war were in need of these goods.

The goods being sold all over the world brought down the debt that had been created during the war, and the U.S. enjoyed ever-increasing prosperity year over year.

Over time, manufacturing practices started to get sloppy, American products became cheaper and something called globalization took hold.

Globalization is the process of interaction and integration between people, businesses, and governments worldwide.

In the 1960's, if you had sat in on a corporate board meeting with a big U.S. manufacturer, you would have been sitting across from Americans, who spoke English.

Now because of globalization, you might need headphones that can translate that English into whatever language the people or corporate officers speak.

So as a country like China buys stock on The New York Stock Exchange or NYSE, and becomes the majority holders of shares in a stock, they also have larger ownership in the corporation and start having more clout at the table and start requesting that these products are made in their country.

Due to globalization, under GATT or (General Agreement on Tariffs and Trade) followed then by the WTO or (World Trade Organization) in 1995 the United States sent many thousands of manufacturing plants overseas, along with millions of jobs, and in the process lost the base of what had made the country strong during the twentieth century: its GDP.

Now the country has lost the majority of its manufacturing base and turned to the idea of a service-based economy. But without the manufacturing base, there's not much money for services rendered.

But the even bigger problem lies in the fact that the government is now doubling the debt on average once every 8 years. Now with so much debt, we can barely pay the interest on the old debt if bond yields Rise by too much.

 The other problem is that Pension funds require yields of 7%. U.S. Treasury bonds don't come close to that. Now pension fund managers are purchasing junk bonds with higher yields to try to make up the difference.

 Junk bonds, or high-yield debt, are bonds that payout higher yields. The reason for this is these are loans given out to so-called high-risk borrowers. Something more disturbing is the fact that the U.S. is running out of buyers for its debt or bonds.

Nations like Russia and China are tired of American Hegemony control everywhere and on every continent of the planet.

Russia stopped buying U.S. bonds in 2018 selling off 84% of their holdings. China is buying less U.S. debt but still has the second-largest holdings after Japan. China only buys our debt so that American consumers can have access to credit.

For without China buying our debt American consumers would have no credit or much less credit and possibly no credit cards to buy cheap products made in China and sold at Walmart or other brick and mortar stores.

In 2008 our national debt stood at $8 trillion dollars.

Since then, we have increased our national debt by $20 trillion dollars.

The money printing, stimulus packages, and (QE) Quantitative Easing since the 2008 financial crisis, Was designed to stimulate our economy but without a manufacturing base, whos economy were we trying to stimulate?

Now future generations owe $20trillion dollars to China so that we could stimulate their economy,

and own cheap clothes that a monkey wouldn't were on a bad day.

Now, CEOs get rich, and we get cheap clothes, and cheap plastic goods that sit in the garage for 3 years till we haul them off to the thrift store.

CHAPTER 2

UNDERSTANDING INFLATION, DEFLATION, STAGFLATION, AND MONEY SUPPLY

Inflation

Inflation is caused in monetary terms on a couple of fronts, first the expansion of the currency supply, and second when the velocity of money increases.

First, let's talk about the expansion, when governments create currency, that currency gets diluted and its store of value becomes increasingly worthless with the printing of it.

The second is the velocity of the currency. Velocity is the measurement of the number of times each unit of currency changes hands in an economy. When citizens

start feeling good they start spending money, which can be healthy. But in a country that has expanded its M1 money supply, as has been done in the United States, things can get out of control in a hurry. In fact, the website of the Federal Reserve, (FRED) stopped showing
the M1 money supply as of February 2, 2021, for obvious reasons.

So what is M1 money?

Understanding Types of Money and Money Supply

M1, Money, represents U.S. dollars or currency in circulation and includes dollars in checking accounts.

M2, Money includes all M1 money supply plus savings deposits and CDs or (Certificates of Deposit).

M3, is M1, plus M2, and including institutional money market accounts.

When someone purchases a home and signs the final document of the loan, they just increased the money supply and debt of the planet.

If that home cost $300,000 they just added $300,000 dollars to the M3 money supply.

Banks then take those mortgages and bundle them together in something called CMOs or Collateralized Mortgage Obligations. These CMOs are packaged together and sold to institutions that repackage them into bonds and sell them to pension funds.

The same thing happens with car loans. When somebody buys a car and they sign the final page of the document on an auto loan, they just expanded the M3 money supply of the planet.

Now that loan gets pooled together with other car loans in something called a CLO. CLOs are Collateralized Loan Obligations. Let's not forget CDOs, (Collateralized Debt Obligations), used for smaller loans, also the same as with CLOs and CMOs.

So every day the money supply of the planet grows because we have a debt-based monetary system. The system turns debt, or bonds, into a form of money.

Banks and central banks love this system because Mainstreet is put into debt servitude. Or a form of bondage where they owe the debt back with interest and the banks give loans with money they never had in the first place. This is called Fractional Reserve Lending.

Fractional Reserve Lending or Fractional Reserve Banking is the system banks use today. For an example, when you deposit $100 dollars in your bank account, the bank can loan out $95 dollars and hold just $5 dollars in a 5% reserve system.

So if somebody brings in $100,000 dollars, the bank can loan out $95,000 dollars.

This system works fine until there's a bank run where people panic and try to withdraw all their money at the same time. This is when the banks declare a banking holiday and won't open their doors.

So it's not just money printing of M1 money. It's all the home loans, car loans, and every other type of loan that expands the M2 and M3 money supply as well.

Today, instead of saving up money to purchase things, people get loans, or a good faith contract to pay it back. This is basically, a bond, That works fine till the economy takes a nosedive and the holders of those bonds, often times pensioners, take a haircut on their pensions.

In years past your grandparents probably wouldn't have gone to the bank and asked for a loan, they probably would have just saved up the money and bought it with cash.

Back then it was a different monetary system based on money, and it was much harder to get a loan, people earned money and it held its value as it was backed by gold, today it's a debt-backed monetary system backed by debt or bonds.

Banks make their money giving out the loans, then package them up into CLOs and pass the debt on like a hot potato to a pension fund so that when the economy tanks, it's not them who take the hit

Thomas Jefferson

Quote in a letter to John Taylor 1816.

"If the American people ever allow private banks to control the issue of their currency, first by inflation, then by deflation, the banks and corporations that will grow up around [the banks] will deprive the people of all property until their children wake-up homeless on the continent their fathers conquered. The issuing power should be taken from the banks and restored to the people, to whom it properly belongs."

"I sincerely believe that banking establishments are more dangerous than standing armies, and that the principle of spending money to be paid by posterity under the name of funding is but swindling futurity on a large scale." –Thomas Jefferson to John Taylor, 1816. ME 15:23

Understanding Deflation

Deflation is the contraction of the money supply.

When interest rates are low, the money flows and banks give out loans. But when the Central Banks raise interest rates and tighten up lending, now the money supply tightens, and Mainstreet scrambles to find an ever-decreasing supply of money in the economy, to pay on the loans granted when the money supply was larger and money was easy.

Now, the banks sit back and collect on the defaulted homes, cars, and other assets that were bought with loans that had nothing backing them to begin with.

Deflation can be healthy in an economy that is not too leveraged with debt, and for individuals that still have a job. As prices at the grocery store will stay the same or go down. The problem is when you run into something called Stagflation.

Understanding Stagflation

Stagflation is all of the above. At the same time, you have a poor economy with rising prices due to currency creation, or currency collapse.

Inflation, Deflation and Stagflation

When the Federal Reserve talks about trying to achieve their 2% inflation target, what they're actually talking about is robbing you of 2 percent of your purchasing power.

The problem doesn't arise when the economy is slow. The problem arises when the economy speeds up and the velocity of money speeds up. You can find yourself in a situation like the Weimar Republic found themselves in. The only difference is we have much more currency sloshing around in the economy now than they had back then.

Now let's multiply the 2% inflation target Janet Yellen and other Federal Reserve Chairman talk about.

Over ten years, that 2% turns into 20%.Now you can start to see how the Federal Reserve System robs Mainstreet of their purchasing power. You see you can't tax deflation but you can tax inflation.

CHAPTER 3

FROM BRETTON WOODS AND GOLD TO THE PETRODOLLAR AND BONDS

Fiat Currency

The United States dollar is a fiat currency that is backed by bonds Or the equivalent of an IOU.

Today most bankers, accountants, and financial advisors think the U.S. dollar is money. They don't understand the difference between money and Fiat currency.

When President Nixon temporarily suspended the convertibility of dollars for gold in August of 1971, our monetary system went from a form of a gold standard to a Fiat currencies system.

Every fiat currency in history has either gone to zero or lost 99% of its purchasing power in relation to gold.

So what then is a Fiat currency. Fiat currency is a government-issued currency that is backed by either bonds or nothing, or bonds that will never be paid back, therefore nothing.

Prior to 1971, the U.S. dollar was money in that it was backed by gold and every $35 dollars was redeemable for one once of gold.

The dollar held its value in that the U.S. had a set amount of gold in its vaults. And therefore a fixed amount of currency that could be created, and it couldn't be created at will by central bankers.

The problem with the dollar today is that as the Federal Reserve prints fiat currency they debase it.

Therefore causing it to lose much of its purchasing power, and without sound money it becomes very hard to have a strong economy.

Today, the dollar is backed by bonds, and in a weak economy, when people lose their jobs, and their means of income they lose their ability to make the payment on their home or car loans.

Now, their neighbor's pension fund that holds that bond could become unstable or even possibly go into default.

A bond is a form of loan or IOU. The holder of the bond is the lender or creditor. The issuer of the bond is the borrower or debtor.

The planet has never seen this amount of debt. Governments around the world are issuing and selling debt.

Pension fund managers are under pressure to buy the debt or bonds that realistically will never be paid back.

Probably most of you reading this right now are baby boomers, and grew up in a time when the economy was booming with a strong manufacturing base that was based in this country. Gross Domestic Product or GDP was strong and the debt to GDP ratio was getting smaller every year throughout the 1950s.

But then a couple of things happened. First, we went off the gold standard. Second, we sent our GDP, in the form of manufacturing, abroad.

This was sold to us as globalization. When actually it was a free-for-all for CEOs and Wall Street to get rich.

Now with less GDP and more debt, we create more debt so we can pay the interest on the old debt.

But that's just federal debt. There's state debt, county debt, city debt, and town debt. That all needs to be packaged up and sold-- bundled together with a little red ribbon on top.

So who bundles this crap up and sells it? That would be Wallstreet. And they make a lot of money putting pressure on pension fund managers to buy this debt or bonds.

Now I'm not trying to put down the bond market. There are a lot of smart investors and economists who like bonds as an investment. But really how much debt can the world's economy absorb?

If countries keep paying the interest on their debt with a big credit card, then we keep robbing prosperity from future generations so we can enjoy a little less prosperity every year.

Okay, enough of this. Now that I've depressed you all, maybe you should just go directly to Chapter 6.

The Great Depression

Your parents saw the depression and hard times. But what they did not witness was a meltdown of their money. What happened instead was a contraction of the money supply.

The Great Depression began in September of 1929. After the stock market crashed, deflation took hold and the economy contracted. The velocity of money in circulation slowed down. And with no movement of money, and lack of spending amongst citizens jobs disappeared.

Back then there wasn't a big credit market, by the way, the credit market and the bond market are the same thing.

Just as the credit market and the debt market are both the bond market just opposite sides of it depending on whether you're the issuer, the borrower, or the bond creditor or lender holder.

Birth of the Bretton Woods System

By the time World War 2 ended, the United States owned roughly 70% of the world's gold. Gold it had received from countries in Europe that would soon become allies.

Having entered the war late. The U.S. asked for and received gold as payment in return for agricultural commodities and military hardware we sent to future allies in Europe.

When the war was coming to an end, 730 delegates from all 44 Allied Nations gathered at the Mount Washington Hotel in Bretton Woods New Hampshire. Between the 1st and the 22nd of July 1944, the Bretton Woods Agreement was signed.

Setting up a system of rules and procedures to regulate the international monetary system.

These Accords established the IMF (International Monetary Fund) and the International Bank of Reconstruction and Development. Today this is part of the World Bank Group. The US, which controlled two-thirds of the world's gold, insisted that the Bretton Woods system rest on both gold and the US dollar.

It was established that the U.S. would hold the world reserve currency and that the U.S. dollar would be backed by gold with $35 U.S. dollars being redeemable for one ounce of gold. All other world currencies would be backed by gold thru being pegged to the U.S. dollar.

The Bretton Woods system worked quite well until the mid-1960s when the system Felt pressure From two fronts. First, Johnson's Great Society, and second the Vietnam War.

 It was becoming increasingly clear to French President Charles De Gaulle that the United States was not honoring the Bretton Woods system and that we did not have the gold to back up the U.S. dollars. And that we were printing dollars that had no gold backing them, so he started asking for gold. Soon after other European nations started asking for gold.

With the New York federal reserve bank losing so much of its gold. Nixon had no choice, but to temporarily suspended the convertibility of the dollar into gold, or so he said, that was fifty years ago.

Birth of the PetroDollar System

In October of 1973, in response to the U.S. supplying weapons to Israel during the Yom Kippur War, Saudi Arabia proclaimed an oil embargo which caused oil prices to rise 5 times.

In response, Richard Nixon had Henry Kissinger and other U.S. foreign advisers come up with a solution in regards to the instability of oil prices and lack of faith that nations had in the U.S. dollar.

 So in 1974, Henry Kissinger was sent to Saudi Arabia to talk to the Saudi Royal family.

An agreement was reached that the U.S. would provide military hardware and support to Saudi Arabia. In return, Saudi Arabia would price its oil in U.S. dollars and take their excess currency and profits and purchase U.S. treasury bonds.

Saudi Arabia then convinced the other members of OPEC (Organization of the Petroleum Exporting Countries), to do the same.

Also in May of 1973, (S.W.I.F.T) Society for Worldwide Interbank Financial Telecommunication was founded to establish common standards for financial transactions.

Now when any country traded around the world they first had to purchase U.S. Treasury Bonds. So that they could trade into U.S. dollars to purchase oil and other commodities under the guidelines laid out under (S.W.I.F.T).

The petrodollar established stability for the dollar for decades giving the U.S. the benefits that came with having the world reserve currency.

But it was still just a currency, a fiat currency that could be created at will, and create as much debt as needed to make corporations and politicians rich at the expense of future American generations.

CHAPTER 4

WHY YOU DON'T WANT TO BECOME A MEXICAN MILLIONAIRE

Now you're probably wondering, what's a Mexican millionaire and why don't I want to become one?

In the 1980s and 90s, there were a lot of wealthy Mexicans who owned stock in the Mexican stock market. The Mexican Stock Exchange, commonly known as Mexican Bolsa, Mexbol, or BMV. This is where the stocks were traded.

What happened was stocks in the exchange were flooded with many freshly printed pesos, courtesy of the Mexican government. These pesos were looking for a place to call home. The stocks absorbed the currency, and stocks kept hitting new all-time highs. Many wealthy Mexicans became newly minted millionaires. The only problem was that these pesos were not only being absorbed by stocks, but also by beer, tacos, gasoline, and every other asset class.

Now, it didn't matter how many pesos you owned because they had lost all their purchasing power courtesy of Mexican politicians that had not studied monetary history and failed to understand what happens when you debase your currency.

But this didn't just happen in Mexico. It's happened in many countries.

The same thing happened under the Weimar Republic in Germany in the 1920's and 1930's, and in Argentina in the 1990's, and more recently in Venezuela.

OKay. Here's the point. Paper assets are priced in paper. If the currency that, that stock, bond, ETF, CD, mutual fund, or annuity, is priced in is devalued and you go to cash out, you can't buy anything because it's priced in a worthless fiat currency.

With all the leverage built into the system thru money printing and derivatives, economist and investors, can't agree on if the stock market will crash. Or if it will crack up, possibly explode up, like nothing anybody's ever seen, all these people thinking they're rich till they go to Mcdonalds to find they've become an American millionaire.

So what's the answer? Simple. Buy assets denominated outside of fiat currency. Hard assets that have value in a dollar world or outside of a dollar world.

An ounce of gold will buy you a suit today just like it would have 100 years ago. Or that same ounce of gold would have bought you a toga in the roman empire 2,000 years ago.

Gold is not concerned about a currency collapse. It's seen many fiat currencies come and go over the years.

But the holders of gold, silver, and other hard assets will always come out the other side a lot better off having maintained their purchasing power.

Gold coins traveled in the heels and soles of many shoes and boots in Europe during WW2 as the lessons from WW1 had made many people in Europe wise to what a little gold could buy when a war came to an end.

Citizens didn't know what their fate would be. But did know that if they could make it to the other side of the war alive it would take them much less time to get back on their feet and get reestablished.

Also, many families buried coffee cans and jars containing gold at nite next to trees on family farms, with the knowledge that invading armies often steel and when the war did eventually come to an end, even if the farm was lost with no public records at least the family could come back to the same tree at nite and do a midnight retrieval of their gold.

Just remember that gold and silver always do accounting for an expanding currency supply.

CHAPTER 5

IS THE STOCK MARKET THE ECONOMY? NO!

Nowadays, the line between a government and a corporation is becoming increasingly blurred.

Also, is the Federal Reserve bank a part of the U.S. government? NO!

 The Federal Reserve is a central bank. It's a private corporation owned by six banks. But, it could be more, due to how secretive it is and how hard it is to find out any information about it. But what we do know is it was created on December 23rd, 1913 on Jekyll Island in Georgia.

As of July 2019, the fed, short for Federal Reserve, has 24 Primary Dealers or banks it loans with. These banks work along with the Exchange Stabilization Fund, or (ESF) for short.

The ESF and primary dealers are known to rig all the markets of today.

Done with derivatives they set the price of stocks, gold, silver, ETFs, oil, and just about everything else traded on a market today.

If you don't believe me, read the book Ponzimonium. It was written by one of the former commissioners of the (CFTC) Commodity Futures Trading Commission, Bart Chilton.

The Fed is under the belief that as long as the stock market is looking good and at new highs, they can sell the public through the mainstream media, that the economy is good.

But not only are there primary dealers buying stocks with this freshly printed currency indebting future generations with more debt. They're doing what's called "naked short selling" on the derivatives market of precious metals, gold, and silver.

This is the practice of selling futures call options of gold and silver to bring down the paper price so that they can buy the bullion or actual gold and silver at a lower price.

They say they're hedging their clients' positions, but all they're actually doing is preventing the paper derivative price of gold and silver from going up.

And trying to create the illusion that the economy is good.

But what we already know from Chapter 1, is that the health of an economy isn't the stock market going up. It's instead a low debt and strong GDP.

Is there any difference between Wall Street banks and the U.S. government? It doesn't appear so. When Wall Street banks fund the elections of both Republicans and Democrats, these politicians give favors back to the banks who help write laws.

In 1992, Bill Clinton was elected president with the help of some big donors. One of the biggest donors was Wall Street's Goldman Sachs. Eight years later, before he left office in 2000, President Bill Clinton signed the

Commodity Futures Modernization Act that basically got rid of the Glass -Steagall Act.

The Glass -Steagall Act was an act signed in 1933 that was brought about to prevent another great depression.

It prevented commercial banks from operating like investment banks, which meant they had to stick with the traditional bank products.

Making money off the difference between what they could borrow money for and what they could loan money out for, or called the spread.

Now it was becoming a free for all in the banking world. Where local banks were getting in on the wall street derivative products. Banks like Bear Stearns were leveraged over 35 to 1 before they collapsed.

Investment products like Subprime loans and Credit Default Swaps helped make Wallstreet filthy rich.

Then once the banking system collapsed from the risky subprime loans and Credit Default Swaps, former Goldman Sachs employee and then Treasury Secretary, Hank Paulson, said we had to bail them out. So the bankers got another big payday. Every employee of Goldman Sachs got a $480,000 bonus check along with the other Wall Street banks.

So how many bankers went to jail? Possibly 35 lower-level bankers.

In 1989, over 1,100 bankers went to jail over the Lincoln savings and loan scandal.

The Lincoln Savings and Loan scandal is also known as the Keating Five, it was brought to us courtesy of Charles Keating in 1984.

Initially, Keating fired the existing management. Then over the next four years he brought in his team who ballooned up the balance sheet from $1.1 billion to $5.5 billion.

Such savings and loan associations had been deregulated in the early 1980s under the Reagan Administration. This allowed them to make highly risky investments with their depositor's money.

When American Continental Corporation, the parent of Lincoln, went bankrupt in 1989, more than 21,000 mostly elderly investors lost their life savings, because of the leverage Keating's new management team introduced. So congress acted and over 1100 bankers went to jail.

After that, Wall Street decided to do more funding of political campaigns. Now, they don't just fund one side of the aisle but both sides and both Republicans and Democrats. Now Wall Street sleeps much better.

In April of 2020, former Fed Head, Janet Yellen said "the Fed Doesn't need to buy equities now but that the Congress should reconsider allowing it".

That was a year ago and now its happening.

So now the Fed creates currency at will and enslaves future generations by indebting them with bonds they owe back with interest. So that the banks can buy stocks in corporations with money they just print at will, the future generations pay the tab.

The Fed now has more control of the corporations now that they have ownership through stocks, and remember that the fed is six private banks.

It's so private that congressman Ron Paul wasn't allowed to know anything about them. And let's not forget the interest owed to the banks for them loaning money that they just created? Sounds like quite a business.

Now, the Fed is buying Fannie Mae and Freddy Mac, mortgage-backed securities, or (MBS) holding over $1.5-trillion of (MBS) making them the largest landlords on the planet. And these 6 private banks that nobody knows who they are got it all for free. What a deal for them!

Thomas Jefferson

quote in a letter to John Taylor 1816

"If the American people ever allow private banks to control the issue of their currency, first by inflation, then by deflation, the banks and corporations that will grow up around [the banks] will deprive the people of all property until their children wake-up homeless on the continent their fathers conquered. The issuing power should be taken from the banks and restored to the people, to whom it properly belongs."

"I sincerely believe that banking establishments are more dangerous than standing armies, and that the principle of spending money to be paid by posterity under the name of funding is but swindling futurity on a large scale." –Thomas Jefferson to John Taylor, 1816. ME 15:23

CHAPTER 6

ENOUGH OF THE DOOM and GLOOM
HOW TO SURVIVE and THRIVE

The author does not claim to have a crystal ball and know the future. And many smart people, economists, and investors have faith in the bond market. But that being said, I'm assuming most of the people reading this book already own paper assets in the form of Pension funds, 401K plans, stocks, and bonds. And are looking for a way to hedge outside of these Assets.

There are a lot of people today who think of gold and silver as an investment but actually what they are is money.

Every Fiat currency in the history of the world has either gone to 0 or lost 99% of its purchasing power against gold. However, when the dollar loses all its purchasing power due to money printing you're going to want to own hard assets.

So what then are considered hard assets? Hard assets are assets that can't just be printed on a printing press by the Federal Reserve.

Gold can't just be created. It takes time and money to find it and mine it. And it's a rare commodity. Silver is mined just like gold and is a finite resource. Land is another hard asset. It cant be created.

Bitcoin is the newest hard asset. Only 21 million bitcoin can ever be mined. More on bitcoin after I talk about gold and silver.

Currency is a medium of exchange, and a unit of account. It is portable, durable, divisible, and something called fungible, which means that each unit is the same.

Money on the other hand is all of those things listed above plus a store of value.

For those of you who already read Chapter 3, you have already heard me talk about gold as money. It's a hard asset that cant be printed. But the biggest reason for owning gold goes back to previous chapters. It's probably not a matter of if but when this bond bubble the biggest of its kind in history pops.

It's made up of all the forms of currency. M1, M2, and M3, stocks, bonds ETFs, mutual funds, (CDs) Certificates of Deposits, pension funds, 401k plans, and derivatives.

Now, you may be asking yourself, ``How big is the derivatives market? Are you ready for this? It's estimated to be over $1 quadrillion dollars.

As the author, Mike Maloney says, gold and silver do an accounting periodically throughout history. They automatically revalue and catch up to all the currency that's been produced.

The last time this happened was in 1980 when inflation got out of hand. Remember in 1971 gold was still pegged to the dollar at $35 an ounce.

But due to the expansion of the money supply, inflation took hold. And by January of 1980 gold hit $850 per ounce. That was an increase of over 24 times in just nine years.

With inflation running rampant. The standing chairman of the Federal Reserve Paul Volcker, started raising interest rates 4% above the inflation rate. And at some point in 1981, inflation was capped with interest rates reaching 20% at the federal funds rate.

 The dollar was strengthened. And silver and gold retracted. But that was when our national debt sat at $908 billion.

It took the U.S 204 years to acquire $908 billion in debt and which included a couple of world wars. Now, forty years later, we've added 29 times that amount.

 As of right now, looking at the U.S. debt clock, our debt stands at $28,548,950,000,000. That's right over $28 and a half trillion.

Now, when gold does an accounting, for that, we could easily be over $24,000 per ounce for gold. Right now gold stands at $1,800.00 per ounce.

Also back then the debt to GDP ratio was around 32%. Today, the debt to GDP ratio is over 127%. This means there won't be any stepping in by a Fed head to raise interest rates and cap inflation.

If we were to raise interest rates too high we wouldn't be able to pay the interest on the debt let alone try to pay it down. Also raising interest rates would cause the stock market to collapse.

Why do we owe interest on the debt you ask?

Oh, well you see the six private banks that own the bank called the Federal Reserve, that nobody knows who they are, want it.

But I haven't talked about silver as of yet.

Silver comes out of the earth's crust at a ratio of about 15 times that of gold. This means that there's roughly 15 times more silver than gold in the earth's crust. This is why historically gold is priced around 15 to 20 times higher than silver.

But as of today, the price ratio stands at 70 to 1 which means silver is highly undervalued.

Also, gold is only used as jewelry and as a store of value. Silver, on the other hand, has many industrial applications. It's used in solar panels, EVs or Electric vehicles, computer chips, batteries, iPhones, and more. Its demand has skyrocketed over the last ten years.

This is in large part due to the demand for solar panels but also its need in electric vehicles.

But also as gold has sat in the bank vaults, silver has been getting used up in industrial applications like manufacturing.

At present, there is currently much less silver than gold on the market. And the time is getting near when a company like Tesla or General Motors will put in a big order on the COMEX and there will be no silver to deliver. Remember Tesla isn't just a car manufacturer.

Tesla's gigafactory 2 in Buffalo, New York, doesn't make cars. They make solar panels, and those solar panels need a lot of silver. Which could trigger a massive short squeeze that would catapult silver prices to rival golds.

In 1980, silver cost $50 per ounce. Since then, we've increased the money supply 29 times --from $908 billion to over $28.5 trillion now. The spot price of silver is now $25 per ounce which is half of what it was in January 1980.

Shouldn't silver fall in line with the expansion of the currency supply and be 29 times higher? Or maybe 29 x 2? Since it's half its 1980 price?

Now it's time to thank Wall Street. Also known as the smartest guys in the room. In fact, they're so smart that they're doing naked short sales selling silver futures call options on the Comex exchange to hold down the paper price of silver.

Remember the spot price is set at the Comex.

Talk about the 4th of July when they cant come up with the silver for delivery, yee ha!

Thank you Goldman and Sachs. This is nothing more than the biggest gift ever given to Main Street.

It's about time Main Street was able to front-run Wall Street. Sorry folks. I'm not going to discuss front running or High-Frequency Trading. But apparently, if you're a Wall Street bank, it's legal to pay off the Securities and Exchange Commission (SEC) and steal from Main Streets pension funds, and 401k plans.

So now your asking what kind of coins should I buy?

When you're talking about actual gold and silver coins and bars, that's referred to as bullion.

Don't waste your time talking to a financial planner or adviser who says he can get you into a mutual fund or ETF (exchange-traded fund) that holds gold and silver. Those products are for suckers. And you don't want to be the guy trying to cash in his mutual fund or ETF and come to find out the paper ETF failed because there wasn't any gold or silver in the fund.

Remember, those are WallStreet products designed to make Wallstreet rich selling them.

Just buy the real thing and not paper! That being said, there are gold and silver mining companies, and those stocks could go to the moon. But don't forget about Chapter 4. You don't want paper assets priced in paper and find you're a Mexican astronaut. Stick with bullion.

At the end of the day, it's about maintaining purchasing power. It's very likely your financial advisor doesn't know the difference between real gold and paper gold. Don't be angry with his ignorance. Chances are he's college-educated and believes what the Wall Street bankers tell him.

BUYING BULLION

Some of the more popular coins are American Eagles, and Canadian Maple leafs but you could also buy generic rounds that carry less premium.

First, the American Gold Eagle is offered in 1/10, ¼, 1/2, and 1 oz sizes.

The American Silver Eagle is only offered in 1 oz sizes,

These coins are guaranteed by the US government to contain the stated actual weight in troy ounces and are backed by the United States Mint for weight and content.

So how and where to buy gold and silver? I would recommend starting with your local coin shops.

Call two or three and compare how much there charging over the spot? By the way, the spot is the actual bullion price.

Then there are three questions you're going to ask:

1. Availability, do you have the coins in stock?

2. What are you showing as the spot price?

3. How much are you selling over spot?

Prices can vary but typically gold sells between $50 & $70 over the spot. And silver is $2 to $4 dollars over the spot. However, as of today Aug 2021 I just paid $6 over spot.

But in a runaway market, like what happened in 1980, all bets are off. Dealers won't have inventory, and you'll have lines around the block at your local coin shops.

I talked to a gentleman at a local coin shop who witnessed it at his store in 1980. He told me about the chaos. It's just like the author, Mike Maloney, talks about. When the panic starts gold will become Unaffordium and silver will become Unobtainium.

 So some of you are probably wondering where to store physical metals. Here are some options. The first is at home in a safe. The second would be at a local bank's vault. The third place would be in a precious metals depository like they have in Utah. Let's talk about each option.

Option 1
The first, is storing at home in a safe. This could be a good option. But you want a good safe, not a cheap safe that can be purchased anywhere.

Find a local safe store where you can not only buy one, but it can be professionally installed. You could also use a gun safe.

Option 2

Second, find a local bank that provides safe deposit boxes.

One of the drawbacks here would be in a global meltdown, are your banks' doors going to stay open? Or are they going to declare a banking holiday where the doors are locked and they instead go out of business? Will you be able to get your assets out? I don't know maybe?

Option 3

The third option would be to store your metals in Utah in a gold and silver depository like Brinks, and no you don't have to drive to Utah. There are a number of them available.

I've used a few, but the one I like best is goldsilver.com. You can order directly from them, and store metals in either allocated or unallocated storage. Goldsilver.com stores its metals with Brinks. Brinks isn't a bank so you don't have to worry about them collapsing in a crisis. Brinks has been around a long time since 1859. If a depository tries to sell you on storage in an unallocated vault, hang up and go somewhere else or just go to GoldSilver .com and store with Brinks.

WHY YOU'LL WANT BITCOIN

Bitcoin is the most secure network in the history of the world!

Now that being said I just saw an article where all these people lost their bitcoin on an exchange!

Did you hear what I said? They lost their Bitcoin on an exchange! Don't leave your bitcoin on an exchange!

In fact, don't even trust an exchange. These are Wall Street people. They didn't grow up on the family farm milking cows. They learned what little values they have from Ivy league schools and Wall Street.

Exchanges are for buying Bitcoin. That's it.

You don't go to your local Cadillac Dealer to buy an Eldorado, buy it, and say "she sure is nice, take good care of her for me." Then leave, as you drive away in your old Toyota!

I'll explain how to secure your Bitcoin in Chapter 9. So what then is Bitcoin?

Bitcoin is a transferable digital token created on the Bitcoin Network in a process known as mining.

Bitcoin mining is done with computers and operates with a predictable schedule. And by Design, a new block is created roughly once every ten minutes.

Only 21 million will ever be mined. Most of these already have been. Approximately 18.5 million as of today.

Once every four years, the number of Bitcoins produced by mining gets cut in half. That's right. Again, once every four years the amount being mined gets cut in half!

As central banks inject crack currency into the economy and explode their balance sheets, Bitcoin operates in the inverse, mathematically becoming a sound decentralized money that cant be manipulated by pigs in makeup.

Alright. What is Bitcoin, and why should you own it? In plain English Bitcoin gets rid of bankers and central bankers. No more 20% finance charges on credit cards and it doesn't lose value like a Fiat currency.

It's a hard asset that is set at a fixed amount of 21 million coins. That's all that will ever be created. Backed by the blockchain and Bitcoin white paper which lays out the protocol.

In Chapter 9, I will explain more about the workings of Bitcoin. But for now, I'm going to explain why you want it.

As I've already talked about, it's a hard asset that is fixed at 21 million coins, so it's the perfect hedge against central banks money printing that is debasing all the world's currencies. Second, it's a great unit of exchange.

One year ago, if you were to go buy coffee at Starbucks and try to purchase it with Bitcoin, it could have taken up to ten minutes for the transaction to go through. This is because Bitcoin was operating on its base layer which was designed for larger transactions. Today we now have something called the Lightning Network.

The Lightning Network operates on the Layer 2 which is an immediate clearing. Now, Bitcoin can be used everywhere people have access to a smartphone and the transactions are immediate.

This is what's driving the adoption of Bitcoin in second and third world countries where their currencies have gone bad.

Why You Want Bitcoin

Twelve years ago, there was a massive problem.
In that, there was nowhere to turn if the trillions, or possibly quadrillion dollar bond and derivatives bubble blew up.

Institutional investors, such as pension funds, mutual funds, and insurance companies, needed bonds that kicked out yield in the form of monthly coupons to keep pensions and their clients' investors and pension funds solvent.

However, that all changed. Bitcoin arrived on the scene in 2009.

It was called a Ponzi scheme, a joke, and even rat poison by Berkshire Hathaway chairman and CEO Warren Buffet.

Brought to us by the person or persons known as Satoshi Nakamoto. Nobody really knows if he's a person or a group of people from the cypherpunk community.

A Cypherpunk is any individual advocating widespread use of strong cryptography and privacy-enhancing technologies as a route to social and political change. All we know is that he was smart enough not to let his real identity be known.

Central banks, governments, CEOs and Wall Street won't be happy as their manipulation and control will soon cease to exist. And they may have to find a new form of work as manipulating markets, charging exorbitant interest rates, and rigging elections, will all become a thing of the past.

Blockchain can be used almost anywhere as a form of checks and balances, destroying all modern-day corruption.

Bitcoin has no location, no address, no CEO, and no Corporate officers. Just the Blockchain and the White paper which lays out the protocol of how it works.

Anyone and everyone can see the blockchain which makes it completely transparent.

The Bitcoin whitepaper was the first document to outline the principles of a cryptographically secured trustless peer-to-peer electronic payment system. It operates on a blockchain protocol where roughly once every ten minutes a new block is created through the process of mining.

Bitcoin mining involves a series of computers set up to solve a math equation and whatever miner solves it first, is rewarded the new block.

As Compensation for their efforts, miners are awarded Bitcoin whenever they add a new block of transactions to the blockchain.

The amount of new Bitcoin released with each mined block is called the block reward. The block reward is halved every 210,000 blocks or roughly once every four years.

Currently, the amount of Bitcoin awarded stands at 6.25 BTC. This is half of what it was a year and a half ago when the award was 12.5 bitcoin.

A Bitcoin whale is an individual or entity that holds roughly 1000–5000 bitcoin. Currently, it's thought that there are roughly 1000 bitcoin whales. The top 100 bitcoin wallets hold around one-third of all the bitcoins held.

Basic mathematics dictates the price.

The supply of Bitcoin on exchanges rose month over month from August 2011 to March 15, 2020. When the available supply peaked at 3,115,880 BTC.

Since then, there has been pressure from two fronts. First, the halving that happened on May 11, 2020. and Second, from institutional investors eating every new block mined. This has put pressure on supply.

Today, there are currently 2,801,515 available BTC on exchanges. According to Credit Suisse, there are over 56.1 millionaires on the planet.

It is known that 4 to 6 million Bitcoin or BTC have been lost. This means 56 million millionaires, will be fighting over whatever is left to be had when they come to the realization that a new monetary system has emerged.

 Millionaires will have to share roughly ¼ of a bitcoin or 25,000,000 Satoshis. This is basic mathematics, nobody who understands bitcoin is selling.

As we speak, institutional investors are buying as much as they can get their hands on. But it's not just institutions, it's countries, too.

Recently, El Salvador made Bitcoin legal tender, the official money of the country. They are the first country to do so, but now Brazil just announced they're looking at doing the same. Soon more countries will follow suit. With no more need for U.S. greenbacks or dollars to do trade, and no more need for U.S. Treasury bonds.

Heres, a look at global debt, bonds, foreign bonds, stocks, mutual funds, ETFs, corporate bonds, and municipal bonds. And let us not forget about derivatives, the ticking time bomb that makes Wall Street rich until they blow up. Taking your pension fund and your neighbor's pension fund with them.

Below you can see some of the highly leveraged assets that will be sold off at godspeed in the next crisis. As money managers seek the security of hard assets, such as Gold, Silver, and Bitcoin.

GLOBAL BONDS, STOCKS, and DERIVATIVES
 TOTAL VALUATION

1)Stocks – market cap	$ 95trillion
2)Corporate Bonds or Debt	$ 10.6 trillion
3)Municipal Bonds	$3.9 trillion
4)Foreign Bond Debt	$7.03 trillion
5)E T Fs	$8 trillion
6)Mutual Funds	$24trillion
7)U.S Treasury Bonds	$46trillion
8) & don't forget DERIVATIVES	$1.4QUADRILLION

Did you catch that $1.4 QUADRILLION DOLLARS?

What are Derivatives?

Derivatives are options or Swaps, such as Credit Default Swaps, Interest Rate Swaps, Currency Swaps, Commodity Swaps. These are bets on which way the market is headed.

Below, I show a pie chart of what this looks like, I don't add the $1.4 QUADRILLION Derivatives Market as that would be all that you would see.

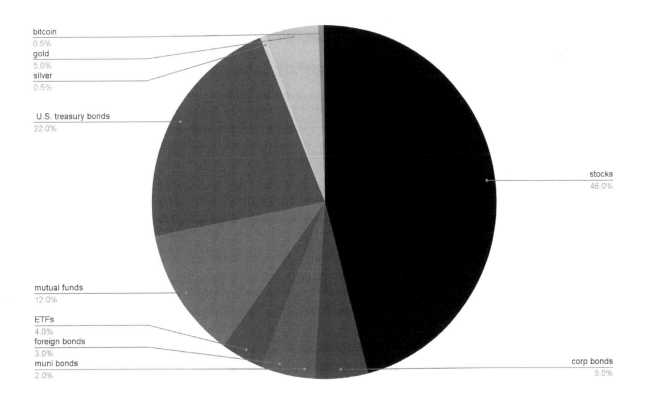

At the top of the chart you see gold representing 5% of the pie with silver and Bitcoin on each side representing .5% each. Bitcoin and Silver are less than 1% but are ready to eat the pie.

CHAPTER 7

CENTRAL BANKS RUNNING OUT OF TIME ON THE LARGEST PONZI SCHEME IN HISTORY

Back in 2008, the world experienced what happens when banks <u>DO NOT</u> operate under the (Glass Stegall Act) they blow up and take Mainstreet with them. I explained Glass Stegall in Chapter 5.

Now, the banks are leveraged with more debt and more derivatives than before. But that's all about to change.

Basel 3

So what's Basel3?

After the Lehman Brothers financial crisis in 2008. Basel 3 was designed. Basel 3 was brought about to ensure counterparty risk didn't spread amongst banks.

The G 20, (countries that make up the 20 largest economies) instructed the BIS, (Bank For International Settlements) Basel committee to come up with regulations to ensure this never happens again.

In October 2014, Basel 3 was agreed upon. Basel 3 takes away the banks' ability to get leveraged up with derivatives. Under the LBMA or (London Bullion Market Association), the Net Stable Funding Ratio Rule requires banks to hold higher - quality liquid assets. In effect, forcing them to get rid of there Bullion trading desk. This is the desk that traded unallocated gold and silver contracts on the Comex. Seven years later not much has happened as it keeps getting pushed back. But that is all starting to change.

Basel 3 is now getting implemented. Over the last two months, the Department of Justice has started making arrests. However, they didn't arrest banking CEOs and top officers. But instead lower-level bankers on the trading floor.

It appears that Basel 3 will likely end the naked short selling or manipulation of the precious metals derivatives market on the COMEX.

There are two possibilities now. (1) the naked short selling stops and gold and silver find true price discovery. Or (2) it doesn't and big manufacturers and investors take delivery of their contracts.

This means that the banks cant deliver on their positions causing the equivalent of a stock short squeeze, or panic buying. Thus, buying back their short calls into a bull run on the Comex the likes of which the world has never seen!

John Exter born (September 17, 1910– February 28, 2006) was an American economist, and a member of the Board of Governors of the United States Federal Reserve System. He was considered to be one of the last good central bankers in that he recognized gold's place in the stability of a monetary system.

Exter created what's known as Exter's pyramid. Exter's pyramid is a graph of a pyramid that's inverted. Its purpose is designed to show, in a time of economic crisis, the financial assets that would be the most ill liquid to liquid, with gold and silver at the bottom absorbing everything as the ill liquid assets collapse.

Bitcoin came along 3 years after Exter's death.

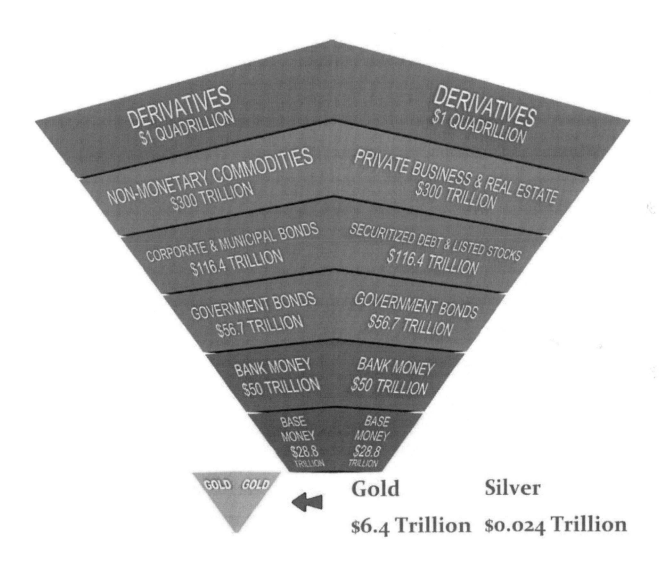

Gold   Silver

$6.4 Trillion $0.024 Trillion

CHAPTER 8

DIGITAL CURRENCY, BLOCKCHAIN BACKED DIGITAL CURRENCY, AND DE-FI

Digital Currency

So what is Digital currency? Digital currency is any currency asset that is primarily managed, stored, or exchanged on a digital computer system, especially over the Internet.

Types of digital currencies include cryptocurrency, Virtual currency, and Central Bank digital currency.

Bitcoin is also a digital currency. Cryptocurrency is a digital currency. But digital currency isn't necessarily a cryptocurrency. It's only cryptocurrency if it is backed by a blockchain and whitepaper that lays out the protocol.

In the last few years, the Federal Reserve announced that it would soon be releasing its Fedcoin.

The Fedcoin will be less a coin, but more an account attached to your bank account.

Now the fed will be able to track all your transactions in real-time and share that information with government agencies.

This is just one of the problems with the proposed digital dollar or Fedcoin. Because it won't be a cryptocurrency backed by a blockchain, but instead a Fedcoin backed by nothing.

Remember cryptocurrency is different from government-backed digital currency. Cryptocurrency has a white paper that lays out the protocol for the blockchain and limits how many coins can be issued.

One more time. Both the Fedcoin and Bitcoin are digital currencies, but the Fedcoin is not a cryptocurrency in that the Fed can create as many Fedcoin as they see fit. Where Bitcoin is limited to 21 million coins. The Fed can create 21 million coins with the click of a mouse in seconds. Then do it again, in effect creating something of no value.

Also, note that babies born yesterday that are in incubators owe $100,000 dollars with interest to the Fed for government projects laid out in 2,700 page spending bills that a speed-reading lawyer couldn't read or understand.

That's the way the spending bills are drawn up. For if congress can't read them then it's ok to approve. With everybody getting their cut from the lobbyist.

However, the U.S. isn't the only Corporation planning to use a digital currency. China released their own version of digital currency in April called The Digital Yuan. Europe just launched e-euro, which is their version of digital currency.

The the only good thing about this is that it's forcing Mainstreet to use and get used to the new technology. Now we come to DE-FI.

So what then is DE-FI?

De-Fi or Decentralized Finance.

De-Fi is what has local banks, regional banks, and central banks, shaking in their boots right now. As banking as we have known it for the last 100 years is getting disrupted.

Decentralized finance creates something known as peer to peer, or a peer to peer network. Where my computer connects directly to your computer. If I want to buy fruit from your fruit stand or buy a car from you, I can do the transaction directly with you and I can bypass the 25% finance fee of the bank or credit card company.

If I'm an immigrant working the fields, I no longer have to lose half my day's wages with a Western Union wire transfer fee when I send my money home. I can now send it for close to nothing.

If I have a savings account at a bank and I am earning close to nothing in interest. Now I can open up an account with a De-Fi Exchange (Decentralized Finance) or (DEX) and earn close to double digits in interest on my money.

De-Fi is based on Blockchain technology. It's like a ledger system that is transparent with checks and balances. When there's a transaction recorded on the Ledger, it's verified by multiple sources making it very difficult to manipulate.

Now, instead of using banks or lending institutions, you will have a piece of software on your phone.

De-Fi couldn't have happened until we had blockchain technology. Blockchain technology underpins De-Fi.

This allows you to have self-automated computer programs that basically operate like a bank, and thus eliminating their need.

To sum it up, De-Fi is faster and Cheaper. It will eliminate the function of banks and exchanges through an app on your phone. Now your bank is on your phone and you won't be hit with a big finance charge.

Heres a few examples of some De-Fi companies

1) Abra
2) Edge
3) Nuri
4) ZenGo
5) Celsius
6) BlockFi
7) Voyager
8) Uniswap
9) Metamask

These are just a few examples.

One of the new blockchain protocols is called Uniswap. Uniswap allows you to swap one token for another token, thus bypassing the need for an Exchange.

Uniswap is roughly 70% cheaper than Coinbase and it's much faster.

Coinbase is one of the largest centralized Exchanges in the world. It has over 1200 employees and took over half a billion dollars in capital to set up.

Within the first six weeks of operating on the Ethereum network protocol, Uniswap was trading as much daily volume as Coinbase. It did it with 11 million dollars of capital and less than a dozen employees.

So now you are all asking whats Ethereum?

Ethereum was released on July 30th, 2015. It is second in market capitalization only to Bitcoin. Founded by a 27 year old programmer named Vitalik Buterin, Ethereum removes the need for lawyers in the same way Bitcoin eliminates the need for banks and bankers.

Now with Ethereum, lawyers are no longer needed. Contracts, or smart contracts, can be made up using ERC-20 Tokens. So what then are ERC-20 Tokens?

ERC-20 Tokens are Tokens built upon the Ethereum Blockchain. Ethereum and Smart Contracts pose a serious threat to Washington and all governments as there will no longer be a need for 2,700 page spending bills filled with gibberish.

But it's not just crony capitalism at risk. Elections will soon be run on the Ethereum protocol with blockchain and public oversight. Now, everybody will be able to look at the blockchain in real-time. And everybody will be able to have one vote, and one vote only, even if your name is John Smith.

CHAPTER 9

HOW TO BUY AND
SECURE BITCOIN

Buying Bitcoin

The first question most people new to Bitcoin ask is: do I have to buy a whole Bitcoin? Answer: NO

You can buy a dollar's worth of Bitcoin, or Satoshis. A Satoshi is the smallest unit of a Bitcoin. One Bitcoin is equal to 100 million Satoshis. Another word for Satoshi is (SATS).

Understanding the Basics

All cryptocurrency has two keys.

1)the Public Key
&

2)the Private Key

The Public key is nothing more than the address of your cryptocurrency. You can put your public address up anywhere--a web page, the side of your van, whatever you want. You can use it to ask for donations or sell products on the internet. You can also have your public key in a QR CODE. Having your public key in a QR code allows you to use it to receive payment. Below is an example of what a QR code looks like.

Think of Bitcoin like a house you live in. You can give anybody the address and they can come to your house. They can slide mail or money through the mail slot in your door, so basically that's your Public key.

Again your Public key is an address. Now for the important key. The PRIVATE KEY.

YOU NEVER GIVE OUT YOUR PRIVATE KEY TO ANYONE !!!

Your Private key is the key to the Deadbolt that nobody but you and your wife has access to. The Private key is how you get into your house.

There's a couple of choices you have when it comes to buying bitcoin: centralized exchanges and decentralized exchanges.

First, here's a list of a few centralized exchanges:

- Coinbase
- Binance
- Kraken
- Bithumb
- GDAX
- Gemini
- Bitfinex

Next, here's a list of a few Decentralized exchanges or (DEX):

- Uniswap
- Kyber

- Ox
- Airswap
- Totle

If you recall, we talked about the difference between Centralized Exchanges and Decentralized exchanges (DE-FI) in Chapter 8. To refresh your memory, Centralized Exchanges use something called (KYC) or Know Your Customer.

Centralized Exchanges basically want to know everything about you, and are going to make you jump through many hoops to get signed up.But once you're signed up, they are fairly easy to use.

Decentralized Exchanges are typically easier to set up but can be more difficult to use.

Now that I've confused you, just open up a Coinbase account and be done with it. They have all my information and the name of my first dog, so you might as well share too.

Second, once you open an account on an Exchange, you need to purchase a hardware wallet!

Sure, you can take the lazy approach and leave your cryptos on the Exchange. This works quite well until the Exchange holding your coins gets hacked. Now the convenience factor is conveniently gone.

Or you try to login to your account and all you get is the little circle going around in endless circles. Or they may say this site is temporarily down for maintenance.

But what they're really doing is taking care of their big clients, the institutional investors, dividing up what coins they have and giving them out to their Wall Street buddies. But don't worry. The site will come back up in a few weeks and you'll find that you were cashed out right before the big run-up. This means they gave you the cash value from two weeks prior to the price run-up and Wall Street received the coins that you thought were yours.

On Wall Street, There's something called Commingling and Rehypothecation. Commingling is like a pooled account of an asset or security. In Bitcoins case exchanges are known to pool them together and Instead of keeping the bitcoins separate, and in separate wallets, they instead get pooled together. Rehypothecation, in simple terms, means multiple parties claiming ownership of the same asset. This is a common Wall Street practice. It works fine until something goes wrong such as a computer hack or multiple people pulling their coins that just so happen to be the same coins off the exchange at the same time.

Securing your Bitcoin

So now that you have an account setup and are buying Bitcoin you're going to want to purchase a Hardware wallet so that you can take ownership of your Private keys. Remember, as it is said in the Bitcoin community, "not your keys not your coins." You don't own your Bitcoin if you leave it on the Exchange.

Now, let's discuss wallets. There are currently a few types of wallets available.

- Software wallets
- Hardware wallets
- Paper wallets

Software wallets are also referred to as hot wallets. They are less secure because they reside on the internet. But they are more accessible and more convenient.

Hardware wallets and Paper wallets are also called cold storage. They stay offline and are less convenient but much more secure.

Most Software wallets are an app that you download onto your Smartphone although there are a few desktop versions. If you're just getting started learning about Bitcoin and cryptocurrency, don't worry about software wallets now. You can always do this later. However, buying a Hardware wallet should be one of your first priorities once you're set up with an Exchange and buying Bitcoin.

A software wallet app is like a leather wallet in your back pocket. A Hardware wallet app is like a safe in your home.

Just as you're not going to go downtown with your safe as you go out for the evening. You wouldn't leave your life savings in your leather wallet on a countertop in your home as you leave for work in the morning and risk someone breaking in and stealing your wallet or your life savings.

So think of your Hardware wallet as your safe and your Software wallet as your leather wallet in your back pocket.

You can load $300 dollars onto the app or Software wallet on your phone and head out for the evening. If you lose your phone you can buy a new phone the next day, download the app and bring up your account where you will retrieve your funds.

Now the important wallet: the Hardware wallet. I've tried a couple of them, however, the one I like the best is called a Ledger. A Ledger is a Hardware wallet that secures your Private Keys offline. I'm not going to go into the details here of how to get it set up. There are many videos on Youtube that explain this already.

CHAPTER 10

PRINTING AT WARP SPEED

Ask anyone what the biggest industries in the world are and they would probably tell you food, transportation, or housing. However, they would be wrong, the biggest industry in the world is currency trading. As governments believe one of their greatest powers is to just print money, no longer do we need manufacturing plants but instead printing presses.

One hundred years ago the First World War ended. Germany, or the Weimar Republic as it was known in Europe, was required under the Treaty of Versailles to pay reparations to the Allied Nations. These penalties stifled their economy and brought it to a standstill. Leaving the country with the same two choices all indebted nations have faced throughout history. Default on their debt, or inflate it away. Defaulting wasn't a viable option as they were completely impoverished, weakened, and surrounded by armed forces ready to take their land.

With their currency no longer being tied to gold Germany decided to pay back their debts with freshly printed currency. Printed out of thin air. This had drastic consequences, and soon Germany's currency lost all its purchasing power. Now, German citizens found themselves needing wheel barrels of currency to go to the market. German citizens started speculating in the stock market, which pushed stocks to new highs. Many Germans found themselves newly printed millionaires.

The only problem with this goes back to Chapter 4 of this book. You might be a millionaire in a fiat currency, but if a million German Marks only buys you bratwurst and beer you've lost all your purchasing power. Below is a chart that shows the currency creation of the Weimar Republic. Take note of the fact that the Weimar Republic stopped accepting marks in redemption for gold before World War I.

Germany

Value of one gold Mark
in paper Marks

Here is a chart that shows the M2 money supply. Note, that the Federal Reserve decided to discontinue the chart as of February 1st, 2021. This chart doesn't include the latest Biden stimulus package.

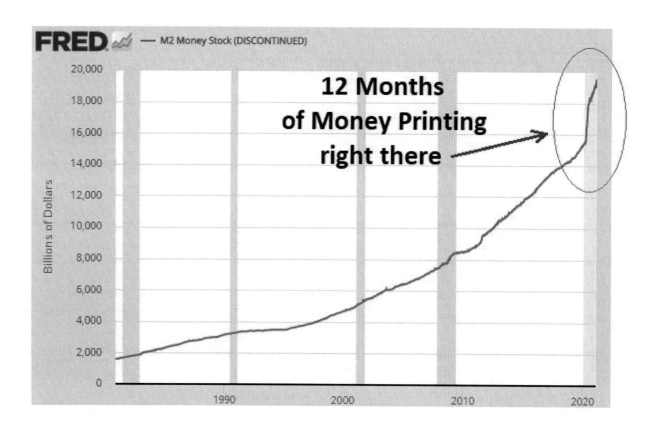

Below, here's a chart that shows the available supply of Bitcoin. Remember from Chapter6 that peak Bitcoin supply happened on March 15, 2020, when there were 3,115,880 Bitcoin on exchanges. Now, the exchanges are running out of supply.

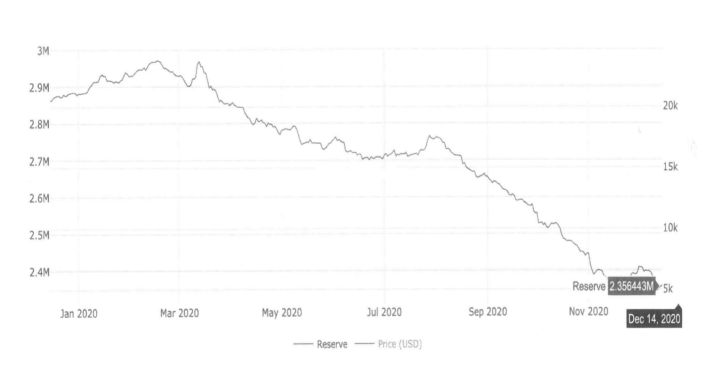

Thus, we have more demand at the same time supply is getting cut.

Now, Coinbase just announced on Sept 28th, 2021 that users can now set up direct deposit by searching for their payroll company or employer through the app.

Last year, Bitcoin payment app Strike announced a feature to convert direct deposit funds into Bitcoin. However, this feature is currently limited to a waitlist of users. This is just the beginning. In the coming months and years, many more crypto and Bitcoin exchanges will be doing the same.

Now, instead of losing 20% or 30% of your annual purchasing power, you can get paid in a digital hard asset with a shortening supply, and increase your purchasing power.

Global adoption

Most people know Elon Musk as the CEO of Tesla, but the largest of his six companies is SpaceX. Two years ago, SpaceX began launching Starlink satellites into orbit. Starlink is a project of SpaceX to build an interconnected network of satellites to deliver high-speed Internet to consumers around the world.

Recently, Musk started hinting that SpaceX will take the network out of beta testing and into global coverage sometime in October 2021. This means that people in Africa, the Amazon jungle, or anywhere else on Earth, aside from the North or South poles, will have Internet available to them.

Currently, there are about 300 million people worldwide who use or have used cryptocurrencies, which is about 3.7% of the total world population.

Global smartphone ownership currently stands at 6.3 billion, with about 80.76% of the world's population owning a smartphone, according to Statista. Bitcoins adoption is increasing on average at a rate of 80% per year, as shown in the graph on the next page.

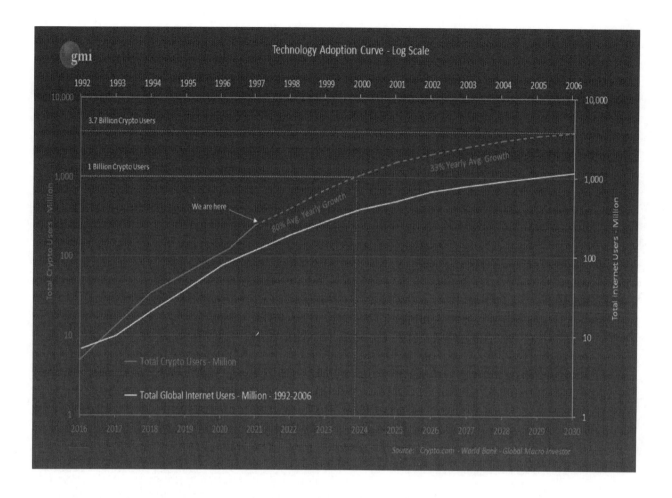

When evaluating new technology, two measures must be looked at, the first being the Network Effect, so this is similar to Metcalfe's Law.

Metcalf's law states that the larger a network gets the more valuable it becomes. So what this means for Bitcoin, is as the global internet becomes more available, and Smartphones become more readily available, banking becomes more available and much cheaper for the rest of the world.

Now, Bitcoins growing from Individuals to Corporations, and now Countries adopting it.

No longer are Countries held hostage to the PetroDollar and forced to buy U.S. Treasury Bonds to acquire U.S.green backs so they can buy oil and other commodities under the Swift Payment System.

Two weeks ago, China announced that it was banning Bitcoin. This is the 18th time China has banned Bitcoin. The last time they banned Bitcoin was six months ago when they banned Bitcoin mining. One year ago China-controlled over 60% of the global mining as they had the majority of the global Bitcoin hash rate. However, now the majority of that mining resides in the U.S.

This will last till the geniuses in Washington ban it, and it goes somewhere else. Bitcoin doesn't care if it's mined in China, the U.S., or Timbuktu, and if you have a hardware wallet like a Ledger you won't care where it's mined either, just that you have access to your private keys.

One week ago, the first Bitcoin futures ETF available in the U.S. was introduced, called The ProShares Bitcoin Strategy ETF.

For anyone looking for no exposure at all to Bitcoin, this is the Wallstreet product designed for you.

Alright. Now, this isn't investment advice but if you have a financial adviser and he tells you he can now get you into Bitcoin with this Wallstreet crap fund, you need to fire him yesterday. Wall Street has been very good at manipulating the price of just about everything for decades.

However, it doesn't matter how many trillions of dollars the Fed gives to their primary dealers to do naked short selling of this ETF.

The primary dealers of the Fed can do naked short sales of gold and silver all day long to manipulate the spot prices down.

However, the price of Bitcoin isn't controlled by the COMEX its instead controlled by the price someones is willing to pay on Centralized, and Decentralized, crypto exchanges, and with an ever-decreasing supply and more global demand good luck to the global corporation known as the Fed to manipulate the price down.

Bitcoin has an open ledger that anyone can see, I'm watching the current block being mined right now on a website called TradeBlock. This is just one of the many sites where you can watch Bitcoin being mined in real-time.

Final thoughts, Bitcoin represents the biggest investment opportunity you will ever see in your lifetime.

Current global adoption sits at 300 million users of cryptocurrency, and 8 billion more that will soon jump on board.

Numbers don't lie and history always repeats. You can't tapper a Ponzi scheme and protecting yourself is easy if you just understand what's going on and what you need to do.

GOOD LUCK.

RESOURCES I

Mike Maloney
G. Edward Griffin
Buckminster Fuller
Paul Hellyer
Catherine Austin Fitts
Robert Kiyosaki
Jim Rogers
David Morgan
Rick Rule
Bill Holter
Doug Casey
Marin Katusa
John Rubino
Gerald Celente
Michael Saylor
Raoul Pal
Jeff Booth
Max Keiser
Preston Pysh
Greg Foss
Lyn Alden
Mark Moss

RESOURCES II

Michael Hudson
Alasdair Macleod
Simon Dixon
George Gammon
Charlie Lee
Athony Pompliano
Tim Draper
Bix Weir
Economic Ninja
Lark Davis
Jake Ducey
Ted Butler
Andy Schectman
George Gilder
Chris Marcus
Dr. Chris Martenson
Danielle DiMartino Booth
Lynette Zang
Robert Breedlove
Tom Bilyeu

Made in the USA
Middletown, DE
25 September 2022

11221345R00055